50 Delicious Mac Dinner Recipes

By: Kelly Johnson

Table of Contents

- Classic Mac and Cheese
- Bacon Mac and Cheese
- Buffalo Chicken Mac
- Lobster Mac and Cheese
- Mac and Cheese with Spinach and Artichokes
- Mac and Cheese with Crispy Chicken Tenders
- Spicy Jalapeño Mac and Cheese
- BBQ Pulled Pork Mac
- Vegan Mac and Cheese
- Mac and Cheese with Sausage
- Cajun Chicken Mac
- Mac and Cheese with Roasted Vegetables
- Truffle Mac and Cheese
- Pesto Mac and Cheese
- Broccoli and Cheddar Mac
- Mac and Cheese with Ground Beef
- Shrimp Scampi Mac
- Mac and Cheese with Sun-Dried Tomatoes
- Mac and Cheese with Meatballs
- Chili Mac
- Mac and Cheese with Ham and Peas
- Mac and Cheese with Mushrooms and Spinach
- Chicken Alfredo Mac
- Mac and Cheese with Sauteed Garlic and Parmesan
- Mac and Cheese with Baked Tomatoes
- Mac and Cheese with Bacon and Asparagus
- Philly Cheesesteak Mac
- Mac and Cheese with Roasted Red Peppers
- Mexican Mac and Cheese
- Mac and Cheese with Caramelized Onions
- Mac and Cheese with Avocado and Bacon
- Mac and Cheese with Kielbasa
- Spaghetti Squash Mac and Cheese
- Mac and Cheese with Smoked Sausage
- Chicken Parmesan Mac

- Mac and Cheese with Sweet Potato
- Mac and Cheese with Roasted Garlic
- Zesty Ranch Mac and Cheese
- Mac and Cheese with Pulled Chicken
- Ham and Swiss Mac
- Mac and Cheese with Sauteed Shrimp
- Mac and Cheese with BBQ Chicken
- Mac and Cheese with Spinach and Bacon
- Grilled Cheese and Tomato Soup Mac
- Mac and Cheese with Sauteed Kale
- Creamy Mac and Cheese with Broccoli
- Mac and Cheese with Crispy Fried Onion Topping
- Mac and Cheese with Roasted Garlic and Herbs
- Mac and Cheese with Cajun Shrimp
- Mac and Cheese with Chicken and Green Beans

Classic Mac and Cheese

Ingredients:

- 1 lb elbow macaroni
- 2 cups shredded sharp cheddar cheese
- 1 cup shredded mozzarella cheese
- 2 cups milk
- 3 tablespoons butter
- 3 tablespoons all-purpose flour
- 1/2 teaspoon garlic powder
- 1/2 teaspoon mustard powder
- Salt and pepper to taste
- 1/2 cup breadcrumbs (optional, for topping)

Instructions:

1. **Cook the pasta:** Cook the macaroni according to the package instructions. Drain and set aside.
2. **Make the cheese sauce:** In a saucepan, melt the butter over medium heat. Stir in the flour and cook for 1-2 minutes. Gradually whisk in the milk, then cook until the sauce thickens.
3. **Add the cheese:** Remove the saucepan from heat and stir in the shredded cheddar and mozzarella until melted and smooth.
4. **Combine:** Add the cooked pasta to the sauce and stir to coat. Season with garlic powder, mustard powder, salt, and pepper to taste.
5. **Serve:** If using breadcrumbs, sprinkle them on top of the mac and cheese and bake at 375°F (190°C) for 10-15 minutes for a crispy top.

Bacon Mac and Cheese

Ingredients:

- 1 lb elbow macaroni
- 1 cup cooked bacon, chopped
- 2 cups shredded sharp cheddar cheese
- 1 cup shredded mozzarella cheese
- 2 cups milk
- 3 tablespoons butter
- 3 tablespoons all-purpose flour
- Salt and pepper to taste
- 1/2 cup breadcrumbs (optional)

Instructions:

1. **Cook the pasta and bacon:** Cook the macaroni and bacon. Drain the pasta and crumble the bacon.
2. **Make the cheese sauce:** In a saucepan, melt the butter over medium heat. Stir in the flour, then gradually whisk in the milk and cook until thickened.
3. **Add the cheese:** Stir in the shredded cheeses until melted. Season with salt and pepper.
4. **Combine:** Mix in the cooked bacon and then stir in the cooked pasta.
5. **Serve:** Top with breadcrumbs (optional) and bake for a crispy finish if desired.

Buffalo Chicken Mac

Ingredients:

- 1 lb elbow macaroni
- 1 lb cooked chicken breast, shredded
- 1/2 cup buffalo sauce
- 2 cups shredded sharp cheddar cheese
- 2 cups milk
- 3 tablespoons butter
- 3 tablespoons all-purpose flour
- Salt and pepper to taste
- Blue cheese crumbles (optional)

Instructions:

1. **Cook the pasta and chicken:** Cook the macaroni. Shred the cooked chicken and toss with buffalo sauce.
2. **Make the cheese sauce:** In a saucepan, melt the butter, whisk in the flour, and gradually add the milk, cooking until thickened.
3. **Add the cheese:** Stir in the cheddar cheese until melted. Season with salt and pepper.
4. **Combine:** Fold the buffalo chicken into the cheese sauce, then mix with the pasta.
5. **Serve:** Optionally, top with blue cheese crumbles before serving.

Lobster Mac and Cheese

Ingredients:

- 1 lb elbow macaroni
- 1 lb lobster meat, cooked and chopped
- 2 cups shredded sharp cheddar cheese
- 1 cup shredded Gruyère cheese
- 2 cups heavy cream
- 3 tablespoons butter
- 3 tablespoons all-purpose flour
- Salt and pepper to taste
- Fresh parsley (optional)

Instructions:

1. **Cook the pasta and lobster:** Cook the macaroni and chop the lobster meat.
2. **Make the cheese sauce:** Melt the butter in a saucepan, whisk in the flour, and gradually add the cream, cooking until thickened.
3. **Add the cheese:** Stir in the cheddar and Gruyère until melted. Season with salt and pepper.
4. **Combine:** Gently fold in the lobster meat, then mix with the pasta.
5. **Serve:** Garnish with fresh parsley and serve.

Mac and Cheese with Spinach and Artichokes

Ingredients:

- 1 lb elbow macaroni
- 1 cup frozen spinach, thawed and drained
- 1 cup canned artichoke hearts, chopped
- 2 cups shredded mozzarella cheese
- 2 cups shredded cheddar cheese
- 2 cups milk
- 3 tablespoons butter
- 3 tablespoons all-purpose flour
- Salt and pepper to taste
- 1/2 teaspoon garlic powder

Instructions:

1. **Cook the pasta:** Cook the macaroni according to package instructions. Drain and set aside.
2. **Make the cheese sauce:** In a saucepan, melt the butter, whisk in the flour, and gradually add the milk, cooking until thickened.
3. **Add the cheese:** Stir in the mozzarella and cheddar until melted. Season with garlic powder, salt, and pepper.
4. **Combine:** Stir in the spinach and artichokes, then mix with the pasta.
5. **Serve:** Optionally, top with breadcrumbs and bake for a crispy topping.

Mac and Cheese with Crispy Chicken Tenders

Ingredients:

- 1 lb elbow macaroni
- 4-6 crispy chicken tenders, sliced
- 2 cups shredded cheddar cheese
- 2 cups milk
- 3 tablespoons butter
- 3 tablespoons all-purpose flour
- Salt and pepper to taste
- 1/2 cup breadcrumbs (optional)

Instructions:

1. **Cook the pasta and chicken:** Cook the macaroni and prepare the crispy chicken tenders according to package instructions. Slice the tenders into bite-sized pieces.
2. **Make the cheese sauce:** In a saucepan, melt the butter, whisk in the flour, and gradually add the milk, cooking until thickened.
3. **Add the cheese:** Stir in the cheddar cheese until melted. Season with salt and pepper.
4. **Combine:** Stir in the sliced chicken tenders, then mix with the pasta.
5. **Serve:** Optionally, top with breadcrumbs and bake for a crispy finish.

Spicy Jalapeño Mac and Cheese

Ingredients:

- 1 lb elbow macaroni
- 2-3 fresh jalapeños, diced
- 2 cups shredded cheddar cheese
- 1 cup shredded pepper jack cheese
- 2 cups milk
- 3 tablespoons butter
- 3 tablespoons all-purpose flour
- Salt and pepper to taste
- 1/2 teaspoon chili powder (optional)

Instructions:

1. **Cook the pasta and jalapeños:** Cook the macaroni. In a pan, sauté the diced jalapeños in a little oil until softened.
2. **Make the cheese sauce:** In a saucepan, melt the butter, whisk in the flour, and gradually add the milk, cooking until thickened.
3. **Add the cheese:** Stir in the cheddar and pepper jack until melted. Season with chili powder, salt, and pepper.
4. **Combine:** Mix in the sautéed jalapeños and then stir in the pasta.
5. **Serve:** Optionally, top with extra jalapeños or a dash of hot sauce for more heat.

BBQ Pulled Pork Mac

Ingredients:

- 1 lb elbow macaroni
- 1 lb cooked pulled pork
- 1/2 cup barbecue sauce
- 2 cups shredded sharp cheddar cheese
- 2 cups milk
- 3 tablespoons butter
- 3 tablespoons all-purpose flour
- Salt and pepper to taste

Instructions:

1. **Cook the pasta and pork:** Cook the macaroni. Warm the pulled pork in a pan and stir in the barbecue sauce.
2. **Make the cheese sauce:** In a saucepan, melt the butter, whisk in the flour, and gradually add the milk, cooking until thickened.
3. **Add the cheese:** Stir in the cheddar cheese until melted. Season with salt and pepper.
4. **Combine:** Mix in the pulled pork and then stir in the pasta.
5. **Serve:** Optionally, drizzle with extra barbecue sauce before serving.

Here are the recipes for the requested mac and cheese variations:

Vegan Mac and Cheese

Ingredients:

- 1 lb elbow macaroni
- 1 cup raw cashews (soaked in water for at least 4 hours)
- 1 cup unsweetened almond milk
- 1/4 cup nutritional yeast
- 2 tablespoons lemon juice
- 1 teaspoon garlic powder
- 1 teaspoon onion powder
- 1/2 teaspoon turmeric
- Salt and pepper to taste
- 1 tablespoon olive oil (optional, for a richer flavor)

Instructions:

1. **Cook the pasta:** Cook the macaroni according to package instructions. Drain and set aside.
2. **Make the vegan cheese sauce:** Blend the soaked cashews, almond milk, nutritional yeast, lemon juice, garlic powder, onion powder, turmeric, salt, and pepper in a high-speed blender until smooth and creamy.
3. **Combine:** Pour the sauce over the cooked pasta and stir until fully coated. Optionally, drizzle with olive oil for added richness.
4. **Serve:** Serve immediately and enjoy a creamy, dairy-free mac and cheese!

Mac and Cheese with Sausage

Ingredients:

- 1 lb elbow macaroni
- 1 lb Italian sausage (mild or spicy), casings removed
- 2 cups shredded sharp cheddar cheese
- 1 cup shredded mozzarella cheese
- 2 cups milk
- 3 tablespoons butter
- 3 tablespoons all-purpose flour
- Salt and pepper to taste
- 1/2 teaspoon garlic powder

Instructions:

1. **Cook the pasta and sausage:** Cook the macaroni according to package instructions. In a skillet, cook the sausage over medium heat until browned, breaking it up as it cooks.
2. **Make the cheese sauce:** In a saucepan, melt the butter, whisk in the flour, and gradually add the milk. Cook until thickened, then stir in the shredded cheddar and mozzarella until melted.
3. **Combine:** Mix the cooked sausage into the cheese sauce and combine with the pasta.
4. **Serve:** Season with salt, pepper, and garlic powder. Serve immediately.

Cajun Chicken Mac

Ingredients:

- 1 lb elbow macaroni
- 2 chicken breasts, cubed
- 1 tablespoon Cajun seasoning
- 2 cups shredded cheddar cheese
- 1 cup shredded mozzarella cheese
- 2 cups milk
- 3 tablespoons butter
- 3 tablespoons all-purpose flour
- Salt and pepper to taste
- 1/2 teaspoon paprika

Instructions:

1. **Cook the pasta and chicken:** Cook the macaroni. In a skillet, season the chicken cubes with Cajun seasoning, paprika, salt, and pepper, then cook over medium heat until browned and cooked through.
2. **Make the cheese sauce:** In a saucepan, melt the butter, whisk in the flour, and gradually add the milk. Cook until thickened, then stir in the shredded cheeses until melted.
3. **Combine:** Mix the Cajun chicken into the cheese sauce, then combine with the pasta.
4. **Serve:** Serve immediately for a spicy and flavorful mac and cheese.

Mac and Cheese with Roasted Vegetables

Ingredients:

- 1 lb elbow macaroni
- 2 cups mixed vegetables (broccoli, bell peppers, zucchini, etc.), roasted
- 2 cups shredded sharp cheddar cheese
- 1 cup shredded mozzarella cheese
- 2 cups milk
- 3 tablespoons butter
- 3 tablespoons all-purpose flour
- Salt and pepper to taste

Instructions:

1. **Cook the pasta and roast the vegetables:** Cook the macaroni. Roast the mixed vegetables in the oven at 400°F (200°C) for 20-25 minutes until tender and slightly caramelized.
2. **Make the cheese sauce:** In a saucepan, melt the butter, whisk in the flour, and gradually add the milk. Cook until thickened, then stir in the shredded cheeses until melted.
3. **Combine:** Mix the roasted vegetables into the cheese sauce, then combine with the pasta.
4. **Serve:** Serve immediately for a wholesome, veggie-packed mac and cheese.

Truffle Mac and Cheese

Ingredients:

- 1 lb elbow macaroni
- 2 tablespoons truffle oil (or truffle-infused olive oil)
- 2 cups shredded Gruyère cheese
- 2 cups shredded sharp cheddar cheese
- 2 cups milk
- 3 tablespoons butter
- 3 tablespoons all-purpose flour
- Salt and pepper to taste
- Fresh parsley, chopped (optional)

Instructions:

1. **Cook the pasta:** Cook the macaroni according to package instructions. Drain and set aside.
2. **Make the cheese sauce:** In a saucepan, melt the butter, whisk in the flour, and gradually add the milk. Cook until thickened, then stir in the Gruyère and cheddar cheeses until melted.
3. **Combine:** Stir in the truffle oil and mix the sauce with the pasta.
4. **Serve:** Optionally, garnish with chopped fresh parsley. Serve immediately for an indulgent, truffle-infused mac and cheese.

Pesto Mac and Cheese

Ingredients:

- 1 lb elbow macaroni
- 1/2 cup pesto sauce (store-bought or homemade)
- 2 cups shredded mozzarella cheese
- 2 cups shredded Parmesan cheese
- 2 cups milk
- 3 tablespoons butter
- 3 tablespoons all-purpose flour
- Salt and pepper to taste

Instructions:

1. **Cook the pasta:** Cook the macaroni according to package instructions. Drain and set aside.
2. **Make the cheese sauce:** In a saucepan, melt the butter, whisk in the flour, and gradually add the milk. Cook until thickened, then stir in the mozzarella and Parmesan cheeses until melted.
3. **Combine:** Stir in the pesto sauce and mix the sauce with the pasta.
4. **Serve:** Serve immediately for a fresh, herby twist on mac and cheese.

Broccoli and Cheddar Mac

Ingredients:

- 1 lb elbow macaroni
- 2 cups steamed broccoli florets
- 2 cups shredded sharp cheddar cheese
- 2 cups milk
- 3 tablespoons butter
- 3 tablespoons all-purpose flour
- Salt and pepper to taste

Instructions:

1. **Cook the pasta and broccoli:** Cook the macaroni. Steam the broccoli until tender.
2. **Make the cheese sauce:** In a saucepan, melt the butter, whisk in the flour, and gradually add the milk. Cook until thickened, then stir in the shredded cheddar until melted.
3. **Combine:** Mix the steamed broccoli into the cheese sauce, then combine with the pasta.
4. **Serve:** Serve immediately for a classic, hearty mac and cheese.

Mac and Cheese with Ground Beef

Ingredients:

- 1 lb elbow macaroni
- 1 lb ground beef
- 2 cups shredded sharp cheddar cheese
- 2 cups milk
- 3 tablespoons butter
- 3 tablespoons all-purpose flour
- Salt and pepper to taste
- 1/2 teaspoon garlic powder

Instructions:

1. **Cook the pasta and beef:** Cook the macaroni. In a skillet, cook the ground beef over medium heat, breaking it apart as it cooks, until browned. Drain any excess fat.
2. **Make the cheese sauce:** In a saucepan, melt the butter, whisk in the flour, and gradually add the milk. Cook until thickened, then stir in the cheddar cheese until melted.
3. **Combine:** Mix the ground beef into the cheese sauce, then combine with the pasta.
4. **Serve:** Season with salt, pepper, and garlic powder. Serve immediately.

Shrimp Scampi Mac

Ingredients:

- 1 lb elbow macaroni
- 1 lb shrimp, peeled and deveined
- 2 tablespoons butter
- 2 cloves garlic, minced
- 1/2 teaspoon red pepper flakes (optional)
- 2 cups shredded Parmesan cheese
- 2 cups milk
- 3 tablespoons butter
- 3 tablespoons all-purpose flour
- Salt and pepper to taste
- Fresh parsley, chopped (optional)

Instructions:

1. **Cook the pasta and shrimp:** Cook the macaroni. In a skillet, melt butter and sauté garlic until fragrant, then add the shrimp and cook until pink. Season with salt, pepper, and red pepper flakes.
2. **Make the cheese sauce:** In a saucepan, melt the butter, whisk in the flour, and gradually add the milk. Cook until thickened, then stir in the Parmesan cheese until melted.
3. **Combine:** Mix the shrimp into the cheese sauce, then combine with the pasta.
4. **Serve:** Garnish with fresh parsley and serve immediately for a seafood twist on mac and cheese.

Mac and Cheese with Sun-Dried Tomatoes

Ingredients:

- 1 lb elbow macaroni
- 1/2 cup sun-dried tomatoes, chopped
- 2 cups shredded mozzarella cheese
- 2 cups shredded Parmesan cheese
- 2 cups milk
- 3 tablespoons butter
- 3 tablespoons all-purpose flour
- Salt and pepper to taste

Instructions:

1. **Cook the pasta:** Cook the macaroni according to package instructions. Drain and set aside.
2. **Make the cheese sauce:** In a saucepan, melt the butter, whisk in the flour, and gradually add the milk. Cook until thickened, then stir in the mozzarella and Parmesan cheeses until melted.
3. **Combine:** Stir in the chopped sun-dried tomatoes and mix the sauce with the pasta.
4. **Serve:** Serve immediately for a tangy, Mediterranean twist on mac and cheese.

Mac and Cheese with Meatballs

Ingredients:

- 1 lb elbow macaroni
- 1 lb ground beef or pork (for meatballs)
- 1/4 cup breadcrumbs
- 1 egg
- 1/2 cup Parmesan cheese (for meatballs)
- 2 cups shredded sharp cheddar cheese
- 2 cups milk
- 3 tablespoons butter
- 3 tablespoons all-purpose flour
- Salt and pepper to taste
- 1 teaspoon dried oregano
- 1 teaspoon garlic powder

Instructions:

1. **Make the meatballs:** Preheat the oven to 375°F (190°C). In a bowl, combine the ground meat, breadcrumbs, egg, Parmesan, oregano, garlic powder, salt, and pepper. Form the mixture into small meatballs and place them on a baking sheet. Bake for 15-20 minutes or until fully cooked.
2. **Cook the pasta:** Cook the macaroni according to package instructions. Drain and set aside.
3. **Make the cheese sauce:** In a saucepan, melt the butter, whisk in the flour, and gradually add the milk. Cook until thickened, then stir in the shredded cheddar cheese until melted.
4. **Combine:** Mix the baked meatballs into the cheese sauce, then combine with the pasta.
5. **Serve:** Serve immediately for a hearty and comforting mac and cheese.

Chili Mac

Ingredients:

- 1 lb elbow macaroni
- 1 lb ground beef
- 1 can (15 oz) kidney beans, drained and rinsed
- 1 can (14.5 oz) diced tomatoes
- 1 packet chili seasoning mix (or homemade chili seasoning)
- 2 cups shredded cheddar cheese
- 2 cups milk
- 3 tablespoons butter
- 3 tablespoons all-purpose flour
- Salt and pepper to taste

Instructions:

1. **Cook the pasta and beef:** Cook the macaroni. In a skillet, cook the ground beef over medium heat until browned. Drain excess fat.
2. **Make the chili sauce:** Add the diced tomatoes, kidney beans, and chili seasoning to the beef. Let simmer for 10 minutes.
3. **Make the cheese sauce:** In a saucepan, melt the butter, whisk in the flour, and gradually add the milk. Cook until thickened, then stir in the shredded cheddar cheese until melted.
4. **Combine:** Mix the chili mixture into the cheese sauce, then combine with the pasta.
5. **Serve:** Serve immediately for a spicy, meaty mac and cheese twist.

Mac and Cheese with Ham and Peas

Ingredients:

- 1 lb elbow macaroni
- 2 cups diced ham
- 1 cup frozen peas
- 2 cups shredded cheddar cheese
- 2 cups milk
- 3 tablespoons butter
- 3 tablespoons all-purpose flour
- Salt and pepper to taste

Instructions:

1. **Cook the pasta and peas:** Cook the macaroni. In the last 2 minutes of cooking, add the frozen peas to the pasta water.
2. **Make the cheese sauce:** In a saucepan, melt the butter, whisk in the flour, and gradually add the milk. Cook until thickened, then stir in the shredded cheddar cheese until melted.
3. **Combine:** Stir in the diced ham and cooked peas into the cheese sauce, then combine with the pasta.
4. **Serve:** Serve immediately for a comforting and savory mac and cheese.

Mac and Cheese with Mushrooms and Spinach

Ingredients:

- 1 lb elbow macaroni
- 2 cups mushrooms, sliced
- 2 cups fresh spinach, chopped
- 2 cups shredded mozzarella cheese
- 2 cups milk
- 3 tablespoons butter
- 3 tablespoons all-purpose flour
- Salt and pepper to taste
- 1 teaspoon garlic powder

Instructions:

1. **Cook the pasta:** Cook the macaroni according to package instructions. Drain and set aside.
2. **Sauté the mushrooms and spinach:** In a skillet, sauté the mushrooms in butter over medium heat until softened. Add the spinach and cook until wilted.
3. **Make the cheese sauce:** In a saucepan, melt the butter, whisk in the flour, and gradually add the milk. Cook until thickened, then stir in the shredded mozzarella cheese until melted.
4. **Combine:** Stir in the sautéed mushrooms and spinach into the cheese sauce, then mix with the pasta.
5. **Serve:** Serve immediately for a flavorful and veggie-filled mac and cheese.

Chicken Alfredo Mac

Ingredients:

- 1 lb elbow macaroni
- 2 chicken breasts, cooked and sliced
- 2 cups shredded Parmesan cheese
- 2 cups shredded mozzarella cheese
- 2 cups heavy cream
- 3 tablespoons butter
- 3 tablespoons all-purpose flour
- 1 teaspoon garlic powder
- Salt and pepper to taste

Instructions:

1. **Cook the pasta and chicken:** Cook the macaroni. In a separate skillet, cook the chicken breasts, then slice them into strips.
2. **Make the Alfredo sauce:** In a saucepan, melt the butter, whisk in the flour, and gradually add the heavy cream. Cook until thickened, then stir in the Parmesan and mozzarella cheeses until melted.
3. **Combine:** Add the sliced chicken into the sauce, then mix with the pasta.
4. **Serve:** Serve immediately for a creamy, Alfredo-inspired mac and cheese.

Mac and Cheese with Sautéed Garlic and Parmesan

Ingredients:

- 1 lb elbow macaroni
- 2 tablespoons olive oil
- 3 cloves garlic, minced
- 2 cups shredded Parmesan cheese
- 2 cups milk
- 3 tablespoons butter
- 3 tablespoons all-purpose flour
- Salt and pepper to taste

Instructions:

1. **Cook the pasta:** Cook the macaroni according to package instructions. Drain and set aside.
2. **Sauté the garlic:** In a skillet, heat the olive oil and sauté the garlic until fragrant.
3. **Make the cheese sauce:** In a saucepan, melt the butter, whisk in the flour, and gradually add the milk. Cook until thickened, then stir in the Parmesan cheese until melted.
4. **Combine:** Add the sautéed garlic to the cheese sauce, then mix with the pasta.
5. **Serve:** Serve immediately for a simple and garlicky mac and cheese.

Mac and Cheese with Baked Tomatoes

Ingredients:

- 1 lb elbow macaroni
- 2 large tomatoes, sliced
- 2 cups shredded mozzarella cheese
- 2 cups shredded Parmesan cheese
- 2 cups milk
- 3 tablespoons butter
- 3 tablespoons all-purpose flour
- Salt and pepper to taste
- Fresh basil, chopped (optional)

Instructions:

1. **Cook the pasta:** Cook the macaroni according to package instructions. Drain and set aside.
2. **Bake the tomatoes:** Preheat the oven to 375°F (190°C). Arrange the tomato slices on a baking sheet, season with salt and pepper, and bake for 10 minutes.
3. **Make the cheese sauce:** In a saucepan, melt the butter, whisk in the flour, and gradually add the milk. Cook until thickened, then stir in the mozzarella and Parmesan cheeses until melted.
4. **Combine:** Layer the baked tomatoes over the cheese sauce, then mix with the pasta.
5. **Serve:** Optionally, garnish with fresh basil. Serve immediately for a fresh and tangy mac and cheese.

Mac and Cheese with Bacon and Asparagus

Ingredients:

- 1 lb elbow macaroni
- 6 slices bacon, chopped
- 2 cups asparagus, chopped and blanched
- 2 cups shredded cheddar cheese
- 2 cups milk
- 3 tablespoons butter
- 3 tablespoons all-purpose flour
- Salt and pepper to taste

Instructions:

1. **Cook the pasta and asparagus:** Cook the macaroni. Blanch the asparagus in boiling water for 2-3 minutes, then drain.
2. **Cook the bacon:** In a skillet, cook the chopped bacon until crispy. Remove and set aside.
3. **Make the cheese sauce:** In a saucepan, melt the butter, whisk in the flour, and gradually add the milk. Cook until thickened, then stir in the shredded cheddar cheese until melted.
4. **Combine:** Add the cooked bacon and asparagus to the cheese sauce, then mix with the pasta.
5. **Serve:** Serve immediately for a rich and savory mac and cheese.

Philly Cheesesteak Mac

Ingredients:

- 1 lb elbow macaroni
- 1 lb ribeye steak, thinly sliced
- 1 onion, thinly sliced
- 1 bell pepper, thinly sliced
- 2 cups shredded provolone cheese
- 2 cups shredded cheddar cheese
- 2 cups milk
- 3 tablespoons butter
- 3 tablespoons all-purpose flour
- Salt and pepper to taste
- 1 teaspoon garlic powder

Instructions:

1. **Cook the pasta:** Cook the macaroni according to package instructions. Drain and set aside.
2. **Cook the steak and vegetables:** In a skillet, cook the thinly sliced ribeye steak until browned. Remove and set aside. In the same skillet, sauté the onions and bell peppers until softened.
3. **Make the cheese sauce:** In a saucepan, melt the butter, whisk in the flour, and gradually add the milk. Cook until thickened, then stir in the provolone and cheddar cheeses until melted.
4. **Combine:** Stir in the cooked steak and vegetables into the cheese sauce, then mix with the pasta.
5. **Serve:** Serve immediately for a hearty Philly cheesesteak-inspired mac and cheese.

Mac and Cheese with Roasted Red Peppers

Ingredients:

- 1 lb elbow macaroni
- 2 roasted red peppers, diced
- 2 cups shredded mozzarella cheese
- 2 cups shredded cheddar cheese
- 2 cups milk
- 3 tablespoons butter
- 3 tablespoons all-purpose flour
- Salt and pepper to taste
- 1 teaspoon smoked paprika

Instructions:

1. **Cook the pasta:** Cook the macaroni according to package instructions. Drain and set aside.
2. **Make the cheese sauce:** In a saucepan, melt the butter, whisk in the flour, and gradually add the milk. Cook until thickened, then stir in the mozzarella and cheddar cheeses until melted.
3. **Combine:** Stir in the diced roasted red peppers and smoked paprika into the cheese sauce, then mix with the pasta.
4. **Serve:** Serve immediately for a smoky, flavorful mac and cheese.

Mexican Mac and Cheese

Ingredients:

- 1 lb elbow macaroni
- 1 can (4 oz) diced green chilies
- 1 cup cooked ground beef or chicken
- 1 cup shredded Mexican blend cheese
- 2 cups shredded cheddar cheese
- 2 cups milk
- 3 tablespoons butter
- 3 tablespoons all-purpose flour
- Salt and pepper to taste
- 1 teaspoon chili powder
- 1/2 teaspoon cumin

Instructions:

1. **Cook the pasta and meat:** Cook the macaroni according to package instructions. In a skillet, cook the ground beef or chicken and add the chili powder, cumin, salt, and pepper.
2. **Make the cheese sauce:** In a saucepan, melt the butter, whisk in the flour, and gradually add the milk. Cook until thickened, then stir in the shredded Mexican blend and cheddar cheeses until melted.
3. **Combine:** Stir in the green chilies and cooked meat into the cheese sauce, then mix with the pasta.
4. **Serve:** Serve immediately for a bold, Mexican-inspired mac and cheese.

Mac and Cheese with Caramelized Onions

Ingredients:

- 1 lb elbow macaroni
- 2 large onions, thinly sliced
- 2 cups shredded Gruyère cheese
- 2 cups shredded cheddar cheese
- 2 cups milk
- 3 tablespoons butter
- 3 tablespoons all-purpose flour
- Salt and pepper to taste
- 1 teaspoon balsamic vinegar

Instructions:

1. **Cook the pasta:** Cook the macaroni according to package instructions. Drain and set aside.
2. **Caramelize the onions:** In a skillet, melt the butter and cook the onions over medium-low heat, stirring occasionally until they are golden brown and soft. Add balsamic vinegar and cook for another 2 minutes.
3. **Make the cheese sauce:** In a saucepan, melt the butter, whisk in the flour, and gradually add the milk. Cook until thickened, then stir in the Gruyère and cheddar cheeses until melted.
4. **Combine:** Stir in the caramelized onions into the cheese sauce, then mix with the pasta.
5. **Serve:** Serve immediately for a sweet and savory mac and cheese.

Mac and Cheese with Avocado and Bacon

Ingredients:

- 1 lb elbow macaroni
- 2 avocados, mashed
- 6 slices bacon, cooked and crumbled
- 2 cups shredded cheddar cheese
- 2 cups milk
- 3 tablespoons butter
- 3 tablespoons all-purpose flour
- Salt and pepper to taste
- 1 teaspoon garlic powder

Instructions:

1. **Cook the pasta and bacon:** Cook the macaroni according to package instructions. In a separate skillet, cook the bacon until crispy, then crumble.
2. **Make the cheese sauce:** In a saucepan, melt the butter, whisk in the flour, and gradually add the milk. Cook until thickened, then stir in the shredded cheddar cheese until melted.
3. **Combine:** Stir in the mashed avocado, crumbled bacon, and garlic powder into the cheese sauce, then mix with the pasta.
4. **Serve:** Serve immediately for a creamy, savory mac and cheese with a hint of avocado.

Mac and Cheese with Kielbasa

Ingredients:

- 1 lb elbow macaroni
- 2 cups kielbasa sausage, sliced
- 2 cups shredded cheddar cheese
- 2 cups shredded mozzarella cheese
- 2 cups milk
- 3 tablespoons butter
- 3 tablespoons all-purpose flour
- Salt and pepper to taste
- 1 teaspoon smoked paprika

Instructions:

1. **Cook the pasta and kielbasa:** Cook the macaroni according to package instructions. In a separate skillet, cook the kielbasa slices until browned and crispy.
2. **Make the cheese sauce:** In a saucepan, melt the butter, whisk in the flour, and gradually add the milk. Cook until thickened, then stir in the shredded cheddar and mozzarella cheeses until melted.
3. **Combine:** Stir in the cooked kielbasa and smoked paprika into the cheese sauce, then mix with the pasta.
4. **Serve:** Serve immediately for a smoky and hearty mac and cheese.

Spaghetti Squash Mac and Cheese

Ingredients:

- 1 medium spaghetti squash
- 2 cups shredded mozzarella cheese
- 2 cups shredded cheddar cheese
- 2 cups milk
- 3 tablespoons butter
- 3 tablespoons all-purpose flour
- Salt and pepper to taste
- 1 teaspoon garlic powder

Instructions:

1. **Cook the spaghetti squash:** Preheat the oven to 375°F (190°C). Cut the squash in half and remove the seeds. Roast the squash, cut-side down, for 30-40 minutes or until tender. Once cooled, use a fork to scrape out the spaghetti-like strands.
2. **Make the cheese sauce:** In a saucepan, melt the butter, whisk in the flour, and gradually add the milk. Cook until thickened, then stir in the shredded mozzarella and cheddar cheeses until melted.
3. **Combine:** Stir the spaghetti squash strands into the cheese sauce, then mix until well coated.
4. **Serve:** Serve immediately for a low-carb alternative to mac and cheese.

Mac and Cheese with Smoked Sausage

Ingredients:

- 1 lb elbow macaroni
- 2 cups smoked sausage, sliced
- 2 cups shredded cheddar cheese
- 2 cups milk
- 3 tablespoons butter
- 3 tablespoons all-purpose flour
- Salt and pepper to taste
- 1 teaspoon paprika

Instructions:

1. **Cook the pasta and sausage:** Cook the macaroni according to package instructions. In a separate skillet, cook the smoked sausage slices until browned.
2. **Make the cheese sauce:** In a saucepan, melt the butter, whisk in the flour, and gradually add the milk. Cook until thickened, then stir in the shredded cheddar cheese until melted.
3. **Combine:** Stir in the cooked smoked sausage and paprika into the cheese sauce, then mix with the pasta.
4. **Serve:** Serve immediately for a smoky, hearty mac and cheese with sausage.

Chicken Parmesan Mac

Ingredients:

- 1 lb elbow macaroni
- 2 chicken breasts, breaded and fried
- 2 cups marinara sauce
- 2 cups shredded mozzarella cheese
- 1/2 cup grated Parmesan cheese
- 2 cups milk
- 3 tablespoons butter
- 3 tablespoons all-purpose flour
- Salt and pepper to taste
- 1 teaspoon garlic powder
- 1 teaspoon dried oregano

Instructions:

1. **Cook the pasta:** Cook the macaroni according to package instructions. Drain and set aside.
2. **Prepare the chicken:** Bread and fry the chicken breasts, then slice them into strips.
3. **Make the cheese sauce:** In a saucepan, melt the butter, whisk in the flour, and gradually add the milk. Cook until thickened, then stir in the mozzarella, Parmesan cheese, garlic powder, and oregano until melted.
4. **Combine:** Mix the marinara sauce and sliced chicken with the cheese sauce, then combine with the pasta.
5. **Serve:** Serve immediately for a delicious chicken Parmesan-inspired mac and cheese.

Mac and Cheese with Sweet Potato

Ingredients:

- 1 lb elbow macaroni
- 2 cups mashed sweet potatoes (about 2 medium potatoes)
- 2 cups shredded cheddar cheese
- 2 cups milk
- 3 tablespoons butter
- 3 tablespoons all-purpose flour
- Salt and pepper to taste
- 1/2 teaspoon ground cinnamon
- 1/4 teaspoon ground nutmeg

Instructions:

1. **Cook the pasta and sweet potatoes:** Cook the macaroni according to package instructions. Roast or microwave the sweet potatoes, then mash them.
2. **Make the cheese sauce:** In a saucepan, melt the butter, whisk in the flour, and gradually add the milk. Cook until thickened, then stir in the shredded cheddar cheese, cinnamon, and nutmeg until melted.
3. **Combine:** Stir in the mashed sweet potatoes into the cheese sauce, then mix with the pasta.
4. **Serve:** Serve immediately for a creamy, slightly sweet twist on mac and cheese.

Mac and Cheese with Roasted Garlic

Ingredients:

- 1 lb elbow macaroni
- 1 bulb of garlic, roasted
- 2 cups shredded mozzarella cheese
- 2 cups shredded cheddar cheese
- 2 cups milk
- 3 tablespoons butter
- 3 tablespoons all-purpose flour
- Salt and pepper to taste

Instructions:

1. **Cook the pasta:** Cook the macaroni according to package instructions. Drain and set aside.
2. **Roast the garlic:** Roast the garlic bulb by cutting off the top, drizzling with olive oil, wrapping in foil, and baking at 400°F (200°C) for 30-40 minutes. Squeeze out the roasted garlic.
3. **Make the cheese sauce:** In a saucepan, melt the butter, whisk in the flour, and gradually add the milk. Cook until thickened, then stir in the shredded mozzarella and cheddar cheeses. Add the roasted garlic and mix well.
4. **Combine:** Mix the garlic cheese sauce with the pasta.
5. **Serve:** Serve immediately for a rich and flavorful mac and cheese.

Zesty Ranch Mac and Cheese

Ingredients:

- 1 lb elbow macaroni
- 1 packet ranch seasoning mix
- 2 cups shredded cheddar cheese
- 2 cups milk
- 3 tablespoons butter
- 3 tablespoons all-purpose flour
- Salt and pepper to taste

Instructions:

1. **Cook the pasta:** Cook the macaroni according to package instructions. Drain and set aside.
2. **Make the cheese sauce:** In a saucepan, melt the butter, whisk in the flour, and gradually add the milk. Cook until thickened, then stir in the shredded cheddar cheese until melted.
3. **Add the ranch seasoning:** Stir in the ranch seasoning mix and season with salt and pepper to taste.
4. **Combine:** Mix the zesty ranch cheese sauce with the pasta.
5. **Serve:** Serve immediately for a creamy and tangy twist on mac and cheese.

Mac and Cheese with Pulled Chicken

Ingredients:

- 1 lb elbow macaroni
- 2 cups cooked, pulled chicken (rotisserie chicken works well)
- 2 cups shredded cheddar cheese
- 2 cups milk
- 3 tablespoons butter
- 3 tablespoons all-purpose flour
- Salt and pepper to taste
- 1 teaspoon garlic powder

Instructions:

1. **Cook the pasta:** Cook the macaroni according to package instructions. Drain and set aside.
2. **Make the cheese sauce:** In a saucepan, melt the butter, whisk in the flour, and gradually add the milk. Cook until thickened, then stir in the shredded cheddar cheese until melted.
3. **Combine:** Stir in the pulled chicken and garlic powder into the cheese sauce, then mix with the pasta.
4. **Serve:** Serve immediately for a hearty mac and cheese with tender chicken.

Ham and Swiss Mac

Ingredients:

- 1 lb elbow macaroni
- 2 cups diced ham
- 2 cups shredded Swiss cheese
- 2 cups milk
- 3 tablespoons butter
- 3 tablespoons all-purpose flour
- Salt and pepper to taste

Instructions:

1. **Cook the pasta:** Cook the macaroni according to package instructions. Drain and set aside.
2. **Make the cheese sauce:** In a saucepan, melt the butter, whisk in the flour, and gradually add the milk. Cook until thickened, then stir in the shredded Swiss cheese until melted.
3. **Combine:** Stir in the diced ham into the cheese sauce, then mix with the pasta.
4. **Serve:** Serve immediately for a savory mac and cheese with a Swiss twist.

Mac and Cheese with Sautéed Shrimp

Ingredients:

- 1 lb elbow macaroni
- 1 lb shrimp, peeled and deveined
- 2 cups shredded cheddar cheese
- 2 cups milk
- 3 tablespoons butter
- 3 tablespoons all-purpose flour
- Salt and pepper to taste
- 1 teaspoon smoked paprika

Instructions:

1. **Cook the pasta and shrimp:** Cook the macaroni according to package instructions. In a skillet, sauté the shrimp in butter until pink and cooked through.
2. **Make the cheese sauce:** In a saucepan, melt the butter, whisk in the flour, and gradually add the milk. Cook until thickened, then stir in the shredded cheddar cheese until melted.
3. **Combine:** Stir in the sautéed shrimp and smoked paprika into the cheese sauce, then mix with the pasta.
4. **Serve:** Serve immediately for a seafood-inspired mac and cheese.

Mac and Cheese with BBQ Chicken

Ingredients:

- 1 lb elbow macaroni
- 2 cups cooked, shredded BBQ chicken
- 2 cups shredded cheddar cheese
- 2 cups milk
- 3 tablespoons butter
- 3 tablespoons all-purpose flour
- Salt and pepper to taste
- 1 teaspoon garlic powder

Instructions:

1. **Cook the pasta:** Cook the macaroni according to package instructions. Drain and set aside.
2. **Make the cheese sauce:** In a saucepan, melt the butter, whisk in the flour, and gradually add the milk. Cook until thickened, then stir in the shredded cheddar cheese until melted.
3. **Combine:** Stir in the shredded BBQ chicken and garlic powder into the cheese sauce, then mix with the pasta.
4. **Serve:** Serve immediately for a smoky, tangy mac and cheese.

Mac and Cheese with Spinach and Bacon

Ingredients:

- 1 lb elbow macaroni
- 4 cups fresh spinach
- 6 slices bacon, cooked and crumbled
- 2 cups shredded cheddar cheese
- 2 cups milk
- 3 tablespoons butter
- 3 tablespoons all-purpose flour
- Salt and pepper to taste

Instructions:

1. **Cook the pasta:** Cook the macaroni according to package instructions. Drain and set aside.
2. **Sauté the spinach:** In a skillet, sauté the spinach until wilted.
3. **Make the cheese sauce:** In a saucepan, melt the butter, whisk in the flour, and gradually add the milk. Cook until thickened, then stir in the shredded cheddar cheese until melted.
4. **Combine:** Stir in the sautéed spinach and crumbled bacon into the cheese sauce, then mix with the pasta.
5. **Serve:** Serve immediately for a creamy, savory mac and cheese.

Grilled Cheese and Tomato Soup Mac

Ingredients:

- 1 lb elbow macaroni
- 2 cups tomato soup (or homemade tomato sauce)
- 2 cups shredded cheddar cheese
- 2 slices of bread, buttered and grilled, then chopped into cubes
- 2 cups milk
- 3 tablespoons butter
- 3 tablespoons all-purpose flour
- Salt and pepper to taste

Instructions:

1. **Cook the pasta:** Cook the macaroni according to package instructions. Drain and set aside.
2. **Make the cheese sauce:** In a saucepan, melt the butter, whisk in the flour, and gradually add the milk. Cook until thickened, then stir in the shredded cheddar cheese until melted.
3. **Combine:** Stir in the tomato soup and grilled cheese cubes into the cheese sauce, then mix with the pasta.
4. **Serve:** Serve immediately for a comforting mac and cheese that combines two classic dishes.

Mac and Cheese with Sautéed Kale

Ingredients:

- 1 lb elbow macaroni
- 2 cups fresh kale, chopped
- 2 cups shredded cheddar cheese
- 2 cups milk
- 3 tablespoons butter
- 3 tablespoons all-purpose flour
- Salt and pepper to taste
- 1/2 teaspoon garlic powder
- 1/2 teaspoon crushed red pepper flakes (optional)

Instructions:

1. **Cook the pasta:** Cook the macaroni according to package instructions. Drain and set aside.
2. **Sauté the kale:** In a skillet, sauté the chopped kale with a little olive oil until wilted and tender. Season with salt, pepper, and red pepper flakes (if using).
3. **Make the cheese sauce:** In a saucepan, melt the butter, whisk in the flour, and gradually add the milk. Cook until thickened, then stir in the shredded cheddar cheese until melted. Add garlic powder for extra flavor.
4. **Combine:** Stir the sautéed kale into the cheese sauce, then mix with the pasta.
5. **Serve:** Serve immediately for a nutritious, savory mac and cheese.

Creamy Mac and Cheese with Broccoli

Ingredients:

- 1 lb elbow macaroni
- 2 cups broccoli florets
- 2 cups shredded cheddar cheese
- 2 cups milk
- 3 tablespoons butter
- 3 tablespoons all-purpose flour
- Salt and pepper to taste
- 1/2 teaspoon garlic powder

Instructions:

1. **Cook the pasta and broccoli:** Cook the macaroni according to package instructions. Add the broccoli florets during the last 3-4 minutes of cooking. Drain and set aside.
2. **Make the cheese sauce:** In a saucepan, melt the butter, whisk in the flour, and gradually add the milk. Cook until thickened, then stir in the shredded cheddar cheese until melted. Add garlic powder for extra flavor.
3. **Combine:** Mix the cheese sauce with the pasta and broccoli.
4. **Serve:** Serve immediately for a creamy, veggie-packed mac and cheese.

Mac and Cheese with Crispy Fried Onion Topping

Ingredients:

- 1 lb elbow macaroni
- 2 cups shredded cheddar cheese
- 2 cups milk
- 3 tablespoons butter
- 3 tablespoons all-purpose flour
- Salt and pepper to taste
- 1/2 teaspoon garlic powder
- 1 cup crispy fried onions (store-bought or homemade)

Instructions:

1. **Cook the pasta:** Cook the macaroni according to package instructions. Drain and set aside.
2. **Make the cheese sauce:** In a saucepan, melt the butter, whisk in the flour, and gradually add the milk. Cook until thickened, then stir in the shredded cheddar cheese until melted. Add garlic powder for extra flavor.
3. **Combine:** Mix the cheese sauce with the pasta, then transfer to a baking dish.
4. **Top with crispy onions:** Sprinkle the crispy fried onions on top of the mac and cheese.
5. **Serve:** Serve immediately for a crunchy, savory mac and cheese.

Mac and Cheese with Roasted Garlic and Herbs

Ingredients:

- 1 lb elbow macaroni
- 1 bulb garlic, roasted
- 2 cups shredded cheddar cheese
- 2 cups milk
- 3 tablespoons butter
- 3 tablespoons all-purpose flour
- Salt and pepper to taste
- 1 tablespoon mixed dried herbs (like thyme, rosemary, and oregano)

Instructions:

1. **Cook the pasta:** Cook the macaroni according to package instructions. Drain and set aside.
2. **Roast the garlic:** Slice the top off the garlic bulb, drizzle with olive oil, and roast at 400°F (200°C) for 30-40 minutes until soft. Squeeze the garlic out of the skin.
3. **Make the cheese sauce:** In a saucepan, melt the butter, whisk in the flour, and gradually add the milk. Cook until thickened, then stir in the shredded cheddar cheese until melted. Add roasted garlic and dried herbs.
4. **Combine:** Mix the garlic herb cheese sauce with the pasta.
5. **Serve:** Serve immediately for a flavorful and aromatic mac and cheese.

Mac and Cheese with Cajun Shrimp

Ingredients:

- 1 lb elbow macaroni
- 1 lb shrimp, peeled and deveined
- 2 cups shredded cheddar cheese
- 2 cups milk
- 3 tablespoons butter
- 3 tablespoons all-purpose flour
- Salt and pepper to taste
- 1 tablespoon Cajun seasoning
- 1 teaspoon garlic powder

Instructions:

1. **Cook the pasta:** Cook the macaroni according to package instructions. Drain and set aside.
2. **Cook the shrimp:** In a skillet, sauté the shrimp with Cajun seasoning, garlic powder, salt, and pepper until pink and cooked through.
3. **Make the cheese sauce:** In a saucepan, melt the butter, whisk in the flour, and gradually add the milk. Cook until thickened, then stir in the shredded cheddar cheese until melted.
4. **Combine:** Mix the Cajun shrimp with the cheese sauce, then combine with the pasta.
5. **Serve:** Serve immediately for a spicy, flavorful mac and cheese.

Mac and Cheese with Chicken and Green Beans

Ingredients:

- 1 lb elbow macaroni
- 2 cups cooked, shredded chicken (rotisserie chicken works well)
- 2 cups cooked green beans, chopped
- 2 cups shredded cheddar cheese
- 2 cups milk
- 3 tablespoons butter
- 3 tablespoons all-purpose flour
- Salt and pepper to taste
- 1/2 teaspoon garlic powder

Instructions:

1. **Cook the pasta and green beans:** Cook the macaroni according to package instructions. Steam or cook the green beans, then chop them into bite-sized pieces.
2. **Make the cheese sauce:** In a saucepan, melt the butter, whisk in the flour, and gradually add the milk. Cook until thickened, then stir in the shredded cheddar cheese until melted. Add garlic powder for extra flavor.
3. **Combine:** Stir in the shredded chicken and chopped green beans into the cheese sauce, then mix with the pasta.
4. **Serve:** Serve immediately for a hearty and satisfying mac and cheese.

www.ingramcontent.com/pod-product-compliance
Lightning Source LLC
LaVergne TN
LVHW081335060526
838201LV00055B/2665